Wind Chimes and Butterflies

Facing the Unthinkable

By Michelle Walker

Dedication

For Mom & Dad, Chris & Kim, John, Nancy, and Michael

The strongest people I know

.

Special Thanks to:

Dan Fisher

Pam Fisher

Mandi Ratchford

Janell Reisch

Christie Rickey

Amanda Wiedemann

Prologue

You deserve to know the truth about me, the fact that I'm not some great author or expert on grief and loss. I'm a Christian from Oklahoma, who in all honesty has been running from writing this book for over thirteen years. I've lost count of how many times I would start writing, then stop, delete it all, and walk away for months only to start again in the middle of the night because I couldn't sleep, just to repeat the whole ugly process over again. I remember, not long after my sister was murdered, I went on a desperate search for books that could help me deal with what I was going through. I would type in various searches on the internet, such as "Christian family member brutally murdered" to see what would come up and never could find exactly what I needed. Oh sure, I found lots of helpful books on grief and loss and a few big titles that everyone had heard of, but nothing that had the upfront and personal experience of a Christian whose life had just been torn apart. I wanted the straight up honest truth from someone else, a firsthand experience of another Christian whose family member had been taken in a violent and brutal way. For me, that family member was my sister, my best friend, and my life has never been same.

After I started writing this book, it didn't take me long to realize why there weren't many books like this. They are just too hard to write. It's painful to relive the details and extremely challenging to find the right words to describe the experiences. It's also difficult to believe I have something to offer when I know there are so many others that have endured worse tragedies. However, the idea of this book continued to haunt me, so I finally came to terms with the fact that writing this may be what God wants me to do. It was time to stop running. Maybe you're reading this book because you know me or my family or maybe you are going through the worst pain and loss you have ever felt in your life and are searching for something, anything to help you through. I hope within these pages, you find what you're seeking because I wrote this book for you.

Now all glory to God, who is able, through his mighty power at work within us, to accomplish infinitely more than we might ask or think.

~ Ephesians 3:20

1

July 17, 2000 was the day that changed my life and my family's lives forever. Maybe you have a date like this as well, one that seems to find you throughout your day, showing up in different forms bringing you back to that moment….that horrible moment. Maybe it's my heightened sensitivity to it or more likely the devil messing with me. Either way, I always seem to check the time at the exact moment the clock says 7:17 or glance over in traffic and see a license plate on a car with 717 imbedded in it. Repeatedly, these little reminders are in my face constantly taking me back to that day, July 17th. The day that I wish I could forget. Sometimes these little reminders bring me comfort, which I do believe could be gifts from the Holy Spirit or an angel. I'm also careful because I believe there are demons out there who seek to mislead and manipulate. Maybe you understand this all too well and agree that these reminders that find us aren't always a coincidence.

I had just returned home from a walk around my neighborhood with a friend, when I received the phone call from Dad. He was letting me know that my sister

Kristie was missing and hadn't shown up to her next appointment. He told me that my mom and brother were already out looking for her when he suddenly got quiet. I clenched the phone waiting for him to say something, and finally he said "Someone's at the door, I need to call you back." It was at that moment I got sick to my stomach and knew that something was terribly wrong. Normally, I wouldn't think much of it because my parents are paranoid worry warts, but I felt light headed and my hands grew cold. It wasn't normal for Kristie to miss a scheduled appointment and not let someone know. She was too professional for that to happen. Kristie had earned her master's degree, and was practicing under her license as a professional counselor, and she had recently been honored with Oklahoma's "Counselor of the Year" award. No, this wasn't like her at all. This time it was different, and I knew it. I started to tremble and I dropped to my knees, kneeling over my couch praying to God that she would be all right. My hands were freezing now from nervousness and my body was starting to shake when the phone rang once more. I didn't want to answer it but I did. On the other end of the line, I heard him take a deep breath and his voice cracked as he said "Michelle, someone has taken your sister's life, and I need you to be strong, because your mother doesn't know yet." I honestly don't remember what I said after that nor do I recall hanging up. My husband was on duty that day and I was home alone. I immediately called the fire station and forced whatever words I could get out to someone on the other end. I don't know who answered the station's phone or what I said exactly, I just knew I needed my husband to come home. I had to get to Mom's house before she got there, but I recognized I wasn't in the right state of mind to drive. Somewhere between my neighbor's house and my yard, I fell down and remember seeing a close-up of the blades of grass in my lawn. Nauseous and crawling, I found my feet again, and scurried to her door, banging hysterically. I look back on the situation now and realize I probably frightened her young children to death, but I desperately needed a ride. She quickly grabbed her purse and took me to my parents' home, which was fortunately only about 10 minutes away.

I immediately noticed the detective's vehicle in the driveway when we pulled up. I don't remember saying goodbye or thank you to my neighbor; I just got out and ran towards the house. As I burst through the door, I was painfully shouting "What Dad, what happened, tell me!?" Dad met me at the door and behind him, sitting at our family dinner table was an unfamiliar face; a detective wearing a navy blue jacket with the mustard yellow words "HOMICIDE" written across it. I couldn't look at his face; I just remember focusing on his hands resting on the table. He wore a large gold ring, maybe a state championship ring of some sort. As Dad was holding me, he said, "A young man has taken your sister's life. Your mom and brother do not know. Please help me be strong for them." I shivered and my voice was wavering as I tried to ask questions. I had so many questions. My hearing seemed odd, like I had water in my ears. I tried to listen to Dad's response to my question: "What did he do to her?" I remember seeing my dad's lips tighten. I could tell he didn't want to speak the words. His voice trembled and in one exhalation he blurted out "He beat her to death with a brick."

"Oh God", I gasped…."Oh God". I tried to comprehend those words, while trying to believe that this was really happening to me. Why would anyone do this to her? She was there to help him. It didn't take long for my imagination to take over as the images flooded my mind of her fighting and being held down while a brick was smashed into her face. Kristie was close to six feet tall with blonde hair and blue eyes. She was attractive, but her love for others is what really made her beautiful. Normally, she worked with children so I was confused. We later found out her murderer was a seventeen and a half year old male; 6 '2" tall and weighing 240 pounds. He was definitely not a child. It's difficult for those who have not experienced such a brutal tragedy to know the feeling that you are trapped in some horror movie and aren't able to escape. Seeing the actual colors outside that are normally so brilliant and vivid, quickly fade to a duller shade. Something changes inside you. I could see the world around me continue to move on like nothing was different, while my world was standing still. I think one of the things that hit me so hard, was that time didn't stop. It kept going and there was nothing I could do to change the events that had occurred. It was so final.

I'll admit, over the next couple days I would tell myself in secret that maybe there was a chance that it was a mistake. I knew it wasn't, but I thought of Lazarus and how he had been dead for four days when Jesus chose to raise him from the dead. Maybe somehow He would do the same for Kristie. I know that sounds crazy but at the time I thought that was a possibility. The questions for God started immediately. I wanted to understand how He could allow such a heinous act to occur to one of His most loyal servants. Why? Kristie was one of the few Christians I knew that had committed her life completely to him and did everything in her power to do the right thing. She wasn't perfect and I knew that, but I also contemplated how many kids and families she could have helped if He had allowed her to be spared. I went through an emotional rollercoaster where I was mostly angry: angry with God, angry with her killer, angry with the angels for falling asleep on the job. I would feel sorry for myself for being left behind in this failing world while she moved on. How could I ever be happy again when she brought me so much joy?

We were very close. Maybe you also have a sibling with whom you share that special bond, a bond that is so much greater than that of a best friend. We grew up just three years apart, with our birthdays in the same month so we shared everything. From playing dolls to shooting hoops on the driveway, we had been together since I entered this world. I realize for various reasons, not all families are close, but luckily for me weren't just sisters, we were also best friends. I had so many plans for our future. She wasn't married yet nor did she have any children, but I had it all planned out in my head. Our kids would grow up together and we would vacation together; life would be perfect. I could call on her at any hour and she could help counsel me and my kids with any issue we faced. It's difficult to put into words the overwhelming pain I felt. All my future events and dreams were stolen- from me, from her, from our family. All of the plans I had for us were gone. I realized at this moment that I was truly not in control. I heard once that if you ever wanted to make God laugh, then just tell him what your plans were for your life.

Kristie's murder is awful in every aspect, but reflecting back, I realize that it could have been much worse. They did catch him and they caught him before he could destroy her body. Some people aren't that lucky.

Their loved one may go missing, never to be found, or when they do get the body back it's decomposed or dismembered past the point of knowing exactly what happened. The human mind is an amazing thing but when there aren't answers to what took place; it has a way filling those empty holes with the most awful, disgusting visions possible. For me, even knowing what occurred, I created my own details and dialogue in my head to fill in the blanks, probably far worse than what actually happened. For me, I had to know. I needed to know. I would relive her last moments again and again in my head, perhaps as a way to come to terms with the fact that she was gone and not coming back. When Kristie's murderer was captured, he had just stopped at a convenience store and filled up an empty mountain dew bottle with gasoline. Apparently, he had plans to burn the car and her body. My family was at least given the peace of getting her back, along with the evidence to prove that she had not been raped prior. I will forever be grateful to the police officers that stepped in and stopped him from stealing that peace from us.

When Chris and Mom finally made it back to the house that day, I wasn't prepared for the reaction. I knew it was going to be difficult, but my heart could barely handle it, hearing my mother's scream and watching her collapse to the kitchen floor in the fetal position. By far, this was the most devastating day of my life, watching my family fall apart. I'm not a doctor, but I do know that our brains have a way of protecting themselves when you go through such an intense shock. That must be what happened to me, because there are many holes in my memory about this day and several of the months following. The next thing I remember is my husband arriving with a look of terror and tears on his face. As a firefighter, he was used to seeing horrible tragedies, but facing them with his own family was an entirely different story.

Blessed are those who mourn, for they shall be comforted.

~Matthew 5:4

2

The next few days seemed to melt together into one long continuous day. I just lingered in a detached state at my parents' house, not wanting to talk to anyone but not wanting to be away from my family either. The local news channels came and went. People were in and out of the house, and flowers arrived, along with tons of food from neighbors and friends. We had so much food we had to take several ice chests to the fire department because we didn't have room for it. The generosity was amazing to say the least. My parents weren't emotionally able to handle certain aspects of the arrangements that immediately needed to be handled, but with their input, my brother, sister-in-law, and I worked together and somehow managed to get through the details of Kristie's funeral arrangements. I don't understand how I was able to do it, but I'd separate myself emotionally at times just to get things done. Writing the obituary, picking the cemetery, purchasing a plot, scheduling with the church and pastor- I had no idea so much was involved in planning a funeral. The expense of it all was eye opening and disturbing as well. Since her death was a homicide, we had a longer wait before the funeral could occur because we had to allow time for all the evidence to be collected for the investigation. I don't remember how long it was before the coroner's report arrived. Maybe it was before the funeral, maybe after but I hated looking at it. I watched Mom flip through the pages, causing all the raw emotional wounds to rip open even further. The page that stood out the most to me was the drawing of a human body and then impact marks and descriptions of all the wounds. I didn't realize until then that she had fought desperately for her life. Seeing the defensive wounds, broken fingers, and extensive trauma to her head gave me a vivid picture of what happened to her. It's one of those things you look at once and then never want to see it again.

When the funeral home requested that we provide her burial clothes, Mom came to me and told me she wanted me to pick them out. "That's what Kristie would have wanted," she said. All these decisions were so hard because, like most twenty-six year olds, Kristie didn't have a will, so we were just doing our best to do what we thought she would have wanted. Kristie had a favorite shirt that she wore all the time. It was a red and blue t-shirt from GAP. I would joke with her about it because every time I saw her she was wearing that same dang t-shirt. I considered the T-shirt as an option but then I remembered how much she loved my wedding dress. She had tried it on a few times and would prance and twirl around in it. She did look beautiful in it. I know that the idea to wear someone else's wedding dress is weird, but to me it made perfect sense. It was the most precious, valuable thing I owned that I could give back to her. It was perfect in the sense that she represented everything God wanted and expected out of His Church, His Bride. That was it. She was God's Bride in my mind. I told Mom my thoughts, and she too agreed that it felt right. I just wanted to give her everything I had. I wanted her to know that she was more important to me than anything earthly. I wish I could have gone back in time and given her my strength, so maybe she could have fought him off. I thought of all the trials that Job experienced and in some ways understood why Job had chosen to shave his head. Was he giving everything of himself away? His strength? Was it his way of showing the world he was grieving? My loss cannot compare to what Job lost but I can say that I understand.

I had driven the stretch of road to her house a thousand times before but this time, I knew when I pulled up, she wouldn't be there in the front yard watering her flowers, nor would she be there to answer the door in a silly manner. As kids, when I would knock on her bedroom door, she would make me answer a series of questions and perform stupid acts before she would authorize my entrance. It was just another way my big sister liked to annoy me. This was something she often did to me even after we had grown up. I would normally just laugh and answer her dumb questions like "what color underwear was I wearing?" Or do ten jumping jacks. This time she wouldn't be there to hear me knock. I would never hear her voice again. We would never sing out loud in the car with the windows rolled down or laugh together. Kristie and I had joked about what it would be like if something happened to one of us. I remember riding in her car on the way home from shopping one day and she said if something ever happened to one of us, she wanted it to be her because she didn't want to be left behind to deal with how crazy Mom would become. I laugh about that now and think that she probably is laughing too. I love my parents, but you have to understand the inside joke here. Mom was and still is the most overprotective parent in the world. Growing up we had curfews, couldn't date until we were sixteen, and lived in a household with no alcohol or tobacco in the house. We didn't have cable TV because it was "dirty." I am lucky to have parents that love me as much as they do, but as a kid it wasn't fun. I didn't always agree with my folks, but in their eyes they were doing what they thought was best for us. I'm convinced that the world would be a better place if there were more parents out there like the ones I have.

I pulled up to her house and saw the lawn was freshly cut and her flowerbeds were blooming. She had really fixed up her home since she had moved in the prior year. Kristie took great pride in being a first time home buyer. She loved the character of her historic home and recently had finished texturing and painting her bedroom and hallway. I thought to myself, "I will get in and out quickly. I will just grab the undergarments that the funeral home needs and then get out." I put the key in the lock and turned it as I pushed open the door. The scent of Kristie filled my nostrils. I had to pause and catch my breath because her perfume still lingered. It took me back to the night before she died. She and I had gone shopping. We were preparing for a trip together to Cancun and were just two weeks away from our flight. She had been so happy because she had finally found the perfect swimsuit. I glanced over and spotted it still sitting in the plastic bag with all the tags attached to it. Oh how I longed to hold her and hug her. I just needed to see her again and talk to her if only for a few minutes. She was my everything. I stopped and stared at her refrigerator door. It was decorated with Bible verses pinned up with magnets. Her dry erase board had a list of people to pray for written in her handwriting. Funny how those personal things such as a person's handwriting can touch you. I reached out, careful not to erase it but I wanted to touch where her hand had been. I paused at her dishwasher, remembering the time when she had run out of dishwasher detergent and thought it would be okay to substitute with the dishwashing soap instead (you know, the kind you would use to hand wash the dishes in the sink). Bubbles overflowed the edges of her dishwasher and flooded her kitchen floor! I laughed and then yelped a cry at the same time. It was painful to laugh, in more ways than one. My ribs and chest felt sore and the thought of laughing made me feel disgusted. On her window sill sat a glass jar, half full of water, with freshly cut flowers from her garden. I had to grasp the side of the counter to steady myself. Get in and out quickly I told myself…yeah right. The sound of my feet walking across the wooden floor echoed through the house. It was odd, because I could feel the lingering of her love here, but there was emptiness at the same time. I knew the Holy Spirit was there with me, holding my hand, helping me through.

God my heart hurt; this was so wrong. My sister was really gone and there was absolutely nothing I could do about it. The finality of the situation was overwhelming. I felt like the angels were watching me, maybe they felt guilty for letting her die. I know some people think that their loved ones look down on them after they die, but I can't believe that. I mean, is that what we truly want? I don't want her to see me grieve. God promises us that in Heaven there are no more tears. If God allowed her to see me grieving, I know her heart would break for me, as mine would to see her grieve for me. No, I know God doesn't want her to hurt ever again. She is in Heaven now and the chains have been broken. She is free and celebrating. I'm truly happy for her in so many ways, but that doesn't change the fact that I'm here and she's not. My tears are really for me, because I can't imagine moving forward with my life without her in it.

I made my way through her home, collecting the items needed and found myself in her bedroom. As I approached the dresser, I noticed her favorite bottle of perfume and I couldn't resist. I carefully opened it and inhaled. I gently touched the hair that was tangled in her brush. I looked at myself in the mirror and just stared. How was I going to go on without her? I walked over to Kristie's unmade bed and climbed in. Curling up in the sheets and covering myself in the blankets, I attempted to get as close to her as possible. It wasn't the same, but the tears flowed and I had to take a moment to let it out again. I needed to go, sure that the neighbors were probably watching the house now and wondering what I was doing in here. Seeing Kristie's favorite t-shirt laying nearby, I make the decision to take it for myself. It still smelled of her perfume so it was comforting to hold against my face. I knew at some point, I would need to come clean out her refrigerator before things started to spoil, but not today. I'd had enough.

I was on my way out when I paused and glanced at her closet door and I felt the need to open it. I knew why. I wanted to look through her clothes to try and figure out what she had been wearing when she murdered. I knew all her clothes so I thought through the process of elimination I could figure it out. Our District Attorney didn't tell me what she was wearing, but I needed to know so my visions of her in my mind would be more accurate. I was surprised when I peered in and found that she had converted it into a prayer closet. There on the floor, was my grandmother's quilt. She had folded it neatly where she could sit and be in His presence. Along the base of the wall were numerous Bible verses that she had printed out and taped up, so that they would be at eye level if she were in a kneeling position. Oh God, she was so good. I was nowhere as committed to the Lord as she. How could He allow this? It should have been me, not her. I knelt down where I'm sure she had been numerous times. I pictured her there, praying, crying, and asking for guidance. All I could do was sit in awe of her faith and weep.

Have mercy on me, O God, have mercy on me, for in you my soul takes refuge. I will take refuge in the shadow of your wings until the disaster has passed.

~Psalms 57:1

3

In many ways, it's good that it took me so long to write this book because I've been able to reflect and see the phases I've endured. I know what it's like to grieve so intensely that the body physically aches and your chest feels like it has a ten pound weight sitting on it. I know what it's like to wonder if you will ever feel the same again. If you can relate to this, I promise you it does get better and the weight will get lighter. Unfortunately, there's no magic pill out there to heal a broken heart. Unless you are under the care of a doctor, I strongly suggest that when your well-intentioned friends and family, offer medication to you, please proceed with caution. I chose to face the storm without pills. I was afraid I might get addicted to the sleep aids or anti-depressants, so I just said "no thank you". It was a harder path, I'm sure of it, but why prolong facing it? Masking the pain wasn't going to make it go away or bring her back. It would eventually surface again so it didn't make sense to me to try and avoid the inevitable. In my opinion, God and time are the only things that really help. I could joke and say cookies help too, because I put on a good fifty pounds in the year after her death. I figured out pretty quickly that I was a stress eater and had to stop that madness as well, because ultimately, when the last cookie in the bag is finished, the pain comes back.

In 1982, at the age of six, I was faced with first death of a loved one. My grandfather's loss had an impact on me, but it was nothing compared to this. I realize that a loss is a loss, but the grief is different when it's from natural cause's verses unnatural. I remember feeling sad that I wouldn't get to hear Pa Pa's stories anymore or brush his hair with his comb, but I didn't cry. Maybe I didn't grasp his death because of my age, but with Kristie's death, I had never cried so much in all my life. My eyes got to a point where no more tears would come. It was like the well had dried up and instead, my eyes would just burn and ache. I never realized that grief physically hurt. I use to think it was all emotional, but now I realize how much more is involved. The whole body is affected. There were a few times when I was driving that I got honked at because I sat through an entire green light. My mind was just somewhere else. I try to have more patience for other people now. It has to be a life or death situation for me to honk my horn because I have no idea what that person might be going through. Maybe he is just a jerk who isn't paying attention or is on a cell phone. Then again, that person may be seriously hurting and going through the hardest trial of their life. Why are we in such a hurry all the time anyway?

I want to sidestep a minute and touch on some of the unusual things that happened to me right after Kristie's death. Things that really made me feel like the devil was toying with me. First, dreams changed drastically. After her death, I only had nightmares for a long while. I used to pray for a good dream with Kristie in it. I wanted to see her face again so badly but instead I would get demon-filled nightmares. One in particular that I have not been able to forget involved me out in the cemetery. I was standing over her gravesite and a sinkhole opened up, causing me to fall down. The demon voices were chanting and all I could see were these green and yellow hands with long fingernails reaching out from the dirt. They were grabbing me from the sides of the hole, pushing me down further into the ground as if they were trying to send me to hell. I have never felt anything so real in all my life. I could smell the rotting flesh and hear their voices. It scared the crap out of me. I woke up and could see red marks on my chest from where I must have been gripping myself. I'm confident any therapist would probably tell me it was normal but it certainly didn't feel normal at the time.   Mom shared with me that she also had nightmares. One I remember her talking about also took place at her grave. She was there, and on top of Kristie's grave was an old hospital bed, just sitting there. I'm not sure what that meant exactly but it creeped me out just thinking about it.

I had a picture that hung right above my bathtub; it was a beautiful door with a flower-filled vine growing over the top. Below it in cursive font was the verse Revelation 3:20 "Behold, I stand at the door and knock, if anyone hears my voice and opens the door, I will come in…" I used to stare at that picture for long periods of time while I soaked in the tub. I would think about how much I would love for the Lord to knock at my door, because I had so many questions for Him. I knew this was not what the verse was talking about but that's what I would think about when I read it.   I'd picture Jesus with his scarred wrists knocking at my door. I would hear the sound in my head of His knocking, and picture myself opening the door to His brilliant face. I really believe demons enjoy toying with us when we are at our most vulnerable point. I think demons hate the fact that I am Christian and would do anything to make me question my faith in the Lord. I use to think that maybe God allowed her to be taken, so I could be tested like Job. Maybe all this wasn't about Kristie, maybe it was about me and everyone else who was spiritually weaker than she was. Maybe He wanted to see how strong my faith really was or wasn't. Kristie was the glue in our family, the one person who held things together. It makes sense to allow her death because He knew her salvation and faith would not waiver. I don't have all the answers, but I do want to share this with you. I think everyone at some point has to ask "Why did God allow this to happen? Why does it seem like other people get divine intervention but she didn't?" I finally heard an answer during church that made sense to me. Christians do not have this superman glow around them, protecting them. In fact, we have a giant, red bull's eye on us because the devil hates us. And who am I to question God anyway? Why do I think He has to intervene for me or my sister?

He already intervened! He sent his Son to die on the cross for me and you. That's all He needed to do. We are saved forever. If the choice was an eternity in heaven or a few more years here on this planet, what would you want? I'm no fool: I'll take eternity please.

I still question God about the manner in which she died. Why did it have to be so brutal? Why couldn't it have been like Elijah and she be taken up to heaven in a chariot of fire? Why wasn't she spared the pain? We aren't supposed to know all the answers but I was able to find peace when I thought of Christ's death. How did He die? Was He spared pain because He was the Son of God? No, He endured more than any of us could ever imagine. He endured the sin of the world. Who am I to question Him? I am unworthy to even ask; I must trust in Him. I like to think Kristie was a martyr. She died trying to help someone else. I know she witnessed to him about Jesus; he just chose a different path, which was obviously the wrong one.

I have found that another challenge in writing this book is staying focused on one thing at a time so I apologize for bouncing all over the place. Let me get back to what I was saying before about the picture on the wall.

One evening, when my husband was at the fire station, and after I had been staring at that picture for quite a while, I fell asleep as I normally would with my dog by my side. I awoke to a very distinct knocking sound. I looked over and the knocking was coming from my bathroom door. I wasn't dreaming. It was loud and direct. It sounded exactly like someone was knocking at my door. All I could think of was that verse. "Oh my God, He's knocking," I thought. I was terrified. I was so scared that I couldn't move. I was such a wimp. I knew I needed to run over and open that door, but I just sat there peering at it from the corner of my covers. The more I think about it, I don't think God would have wanted to scare me. It had to be the devil messing with me. I don't remember falling asleep but the next morning I got up and immediately looked at the door. The sunshine was coming through the windows so I finally got up the courage to open the door. I did it quickly and ran back as the door swung open but there was nothing there. I often wonder if it was a test of some sort, and I can tell you this, if it was then I flunked it big time.

About a year later I finally got my wish, a dream in which my sister was present. I was sitting in an unfamiliar diner, when heard the bell on the door jingle signaling someone entering. When I looked up, there she was, beautiful and smiling. She gracefully walked over to my booth and sat down across from me. We didn't speak. I just looked at her and she looked at me; then she gently leaned over and kissed me peacefully on my lips which caused me to wake up. I quickly tried to go back to sleep hoping I'd fall back into the dream but I couldn't. I knew this was special because I don't ever recall my sister kissing me on the lips in real life. She and I both would have thought that was creepy. I've analyzed that dream a million times and finally have just taken it for what it was...a blessing.

Rejoice always, pray continually, and give thanks in all circumstances; for this is God's will for you in Christ Jesus.

~1 Thessalonians 5:16-18

4

I've always heard that after a major tragedy, people shouldn't make any major life decisions for at least two years. I have to agree with that because honestly, we just aren't thinking straight. We may feel normal at the time, but trust me, just wait. So if you are considering selling your house, quitting your job, moving away, taking your life savings and donating it to a good cause...I'm going to suggest you just sleep on those ideas for a while and give yourself time to recover. You do what you need to do to get through. Sometimes you just have to find something else to keep you busy so your mind has a place to focus. I know everyone in my family had something they did to occupy their time. I think it was about a year after her death, my parents started collecting Hallmark Kiddie Cars. They spent quite a bit of money and time traveling to collect all of these priceless items. More importantly, it allowed their minds to focus on something else, something fun.

For me, it was about six months when I woke up and decided I was going to get a puppy. I thumbed through the paper and found an ad for a breeder nearby, grabbed my car keys and then spent $75 on a rat terrier puppy. It really was the best $75 I've ever spent. My husband was surprised when I walked through the door holding a puppy, but luckily he smiled and accepted her immediately. Through thick and thin, Cleo was there. She knew when I was sad and she never complained that I cried too much or talked too much about my sister. She was always there for me. In my mind, I thought she was secretly an angel who just wore a dog suit. Somewhere in that fur was a zipper I was sure of it! Cleo recently passed and it was hard. I felt like I was losing a family member all over again, but I'm forever thankful that God blessed me with her life.

My brother is an interesting character. He busied himself by accumulating projects. Whether it was a new hobby of bicycling or a new vintage car to restore, he found somewhere else to land his mind and focus. I think it's important to do that because if you allow yourself to think about the tragedy 24 hours a day, it's not healthy. There's a part of you that may feel guilty for doing that, and you may tell yourself that it's not okay to move on. It will feel like you are somehow betraying your loved one for not wallowing in the grief all the time. You can't allow yourself to think this way. Your loved one would not want you to be miserable. You have to allow yourself to live again.

I know what you're wondering… "Am I ever really going to be happy again?" Maybe you're at a point that you don't like to smile or you hate the sound of people laughing. I understand that completely. The honest truth is that everyone in my family handled the grieving process differently. Mom and I grieved more similarly than my father and brother, but we were all still very different. Mom couldn't listen to music for over two years because she said it was too hard, too painful, yet I was the opposite. Music was the fuel I needed to make it through the day. I would listen to my Christian radio station, KLOVE, every day. I found healing in the lyrics from Third Day and so many other artists. I'd cry my eyes out during my commute to and from work but I knew there was healing there, which I desperately needed. Another big difference was how we felt about the cemetery. Kristie was laid to rest not far from where I lived, so I was there every day, sometimes twice a day. I know she wasn't there, it was just her empty shell but I still felt peace when I was there. If it had been left up to me, I would have slept out there. I devoted time to neatly manicuring her plot, fertilizing the grass, & cleaning the headstone. I wanted to make sure everyone that drove by and saw the huge flowers and decorations knew that she was loved. I got to know a few familiar faces at the cemetery, of others who were going through the same thing. An elderly man would come and bring a chair and sit by his wife's grave every day. We'd wave to each other. We wouldn't have to say a word; we just knew that we were both hurting. Nearby in a tree, I hung a wind chime that made the most peaceful music while it swayed in the breeze. There is one thing I miss about the time soon following the loss of a loved one, it's how everything is in focus. The things that really mattered were so clear. The sound of that wind chime was beautiful. I'd heard wind chimes before and even thought they were annoying, but not now. This time it was more spiritual, like heaven was speaking to me. Cheeeeeng chaaaaang, Cheeeeeng Chaaaaaang! Over and over it chimed. The sound was so clear, so crisp. The birds in the sky, an occasional dragonfly, and the butterflies somehow took on more meaning than they ever had before. I would watch as the monarch would flutter, almost dancing in sync with the wind, and when it would choose to land on my hand, it was magical. I would talk to Kristie there, and sometimes have lunch. With time I was more comfortable not going to the cemetery as often, and now I am okay with visiting there just on occasion. I know Mom is the same way. She and I liked going there, but I know my brother really disliked the idea. He was there at her graveside burial and maybe has visited a few times, but he didn't really understand our need to visit her grave. And you know what? That is okay. It does not mean he loves her any less or that I love her any more. We are just different. When you can learn to accept each other's differences, then you have taken a step forward. Dad would come to the cemetery with Mom but I'm not sure he would have if she hadn't made him. He always tried to be strong. He cried, but not as much as Mother thought he should. She would get mad at him for not crying when she was crying or sometimes she would tell me she didn't feel like he cried enough. I know that sounds really crazy but in her defense we were all sensitive at the time. There is some truth in the old saying that misery loves company. I honestly think he bottled it up and then when he couldn't take it anymore, something would trigger a meltdown like a commercial on TV or something unimportant like that. Dad was just as fragile as the rest of us.

The meltdowns just happened. They happened to all of us and they still do. In the journey of grief, sometimes you just have one of those days. I had to learn to take it one day at a time. Kristie always said that happiness was a choice and I believe that. I knew I would never be the same nor would I ever have that special joy that she brought to me but I could be happy, if I chose to be. It would be different, but it was my choice. You will have to make that choice. I cannot do it for you. You either choose to feel sorry for yourself and wallow in your self-pity, or you choose to think about something more positive and choose life. I remember having to say the words out loud "My sister is dead, my sister is dead, my sister is dead" and how weird it felt to say it. I had to say the words to convince myself that it was real. It got to a point that I would talk to myself when I woke up. I'd say out loud "Get up Michelle, your sister is still dead today, you have to get up, there are things that you have to get done." I had to start by taking it one minute at a time, building up to a day and so on. Time is going to march on with or without you. Take comfort knowing that with Christ, nothing is impossible.

Therefore, since we are surrounded by such a great cloud of witnesses, let us throw off everything that hinders and the sin that so easily entangles. And let us run with perseverance the race marked out for us, fixing our eyes on Jesus, the pioneer and perfecter of faith. For the joy set before him he endured the cross, scorning its shame, and sat down at the right hand of the throne of God.

~Hebrews 12:1-2

5

Kristie only had her new car for about a month when she was killed and I remember how proud she was of her white Toyota Camry. She had no idea that her body would someday be in the trunk covered in her blood. The day they released the car back to us, Dad and I had to go downtown to pick it up. I told him I would drive it. When we arrived, I wasn't expecting to see it covered in black. The detectives had dusted the entire car for fingerprints and I guess it was normal to not wash it before giving it back to the family. Fortunately, we had close friends and family that offered to take the car and detail it for us. They knew we would need to sell the car and didn't want us to have to clean the trunk area which was stained with her blood. As I drove the car to their garage, I couldn't help but picture him in the seat, driving. Maybe her murderer was listening to the radio or the Christian cd she had been playing. Did he roll down the windows to feel the wind on his face? Did he try on her sunglasses? I was disgusted. I was filled with so much hate I could hardly stand it. When we came back to pick up the car, it looked like new. They popped the trunk and I had to force myself to peek in and see that the carpet had been replaced. There were also personal items in her trunk and I was dreading the task of going through them. Kristie had such a giving heart. Often times, she would give baby food, clothing, and toys to her clients. As I was going through the trunk I came across a plastic tub that was full of baby cereal and newborn products. It was my sister's dried blood on the outside of the container that caught my eye. I ran my finger across it, knowing it must have been overlooked. I thought of her love for others and then her spilled blood. It made me think of Jesus and how much He suffered and how His blood was shed for mine. Kristie's car was another one of those little things that haunted me. It seemed like no matter where I went or what I did, there was a white Toyota Camry there to park beside me. It happened so often that I had to laugh. I kid you not, one time I had one parked on both sides of me and in front of me. I realize the Camry model is popular but there were days I really had to wonder who was messing with me.

Going back to work was awkward. I honestly don't remember how much time I had taken off after it happened, maybe a month or two but I had to go back.

Like everyone else, I had bills that had to be paid and I yearned for the feeling of normalcy. I didn't want to go back because I knew that everyone would look at me a little bit differently. Things had changed. I was no longer Michelle Walker. I was the girl whose sister was murdered and whose family had been on TV and in the papers the last month. People really do mean well, but I was a little surprised that I was avoided like the plague. I guess when they don't know what to say to someone, people choose to say nothing at all. I understood because I might have done the same thing but there were days that I wanted to talk about it. Luckily I had one or two close friends at work that would talk to me and tolerate my constant grief. I am thankful for my friends because they have been imperative in the healing process. It was difficult to focus at work but I had to start somewhere. I found peace in having something else to think about. It was an escape from reality. But there were still those moments when I would just stare out the window and think about the day she died. I remember that day at work: walking out to my car that evening, thinking what a beautiful day it was, when just a short time earlier, probably while I was sitting at my desk doing something unimportant, my sister was fighting for her life.   Little did I know, later that day I would be given the most devastating news of my life.

It's inevitable that at some point you will have to face the holidays. The first Thanksgiving, Christmas, and birthday without your loved one are brutal. It's like pouring lemon juice on an open wound.   All the traditions we had were ruined. I remember our first Thanksgiving without her was just empty. Mom didn't feel like cooking so we went out to a restaurant and managed to swallow what we ordered. I had never eaten at a restaurant for a holiday in my life until that year.   Normally, Mom cooked all day and we all gathered at her house, filling it full of love and laughter. There we all were, sitting in a restaurant with food that had been sitting under a heat lamp most of the day. I guess the only positive thing to say about it was we survived. I watched other families around us as they carried on, not realizing how much they took for granted and how quickly life could change in the blink of an eye.

Christmas was worse. I'm trying not to sound like such a downer here, but there's really not a good way to say how horrible I felt on Christmas. After Christmas in

1999, Kristie and I had gotten out early to find some good sales. I remember the details of the day and how she carefully picked out her Christmas cards. She looked over all the boxes of cards and told me how sad she felt because only a few of them actually mentioned Jesus and the true meaning of Christmas. She told me her cards would always have Jesus on them. I felt guilty as I looked down at the cards I had selected. I didn't think about the importance of the cards. I had just grabbed the shiniest, prettiest ones. She was my teacher that day and many other days. Kristie did more than talk the talk. She walked it, she lived it, and she died for it. That first Christmas without her, I mailed out the cards she had purchased. Every Christmas thereafter when buying cards, I pay attention...very close attention to what they say. Many times those cards speak more about who you are and what you believe in so I try not to disappoint her. I'm not sure how many years it took before I started putting my tree back up. Christmas was her favorite holiday and not a Christmas goes by that I don't think about her. She and I acted like kids all the way up to the point when I got married in 1998. We used to slumber party at Mom & Dad's house and they would fill our stockings like we were still six years old. We'd wake up at 4 A.M. and run in the living room to see what we got. We just didn't want to grow up. Now each holiday gets a little easier than the last. Our family has done our best to make new traditions and Mom eventually started cooking again. She mentions every year how small our family feels now. It's just not the same without Kristie, but we have to move forward. There was a quote out of the movie *Shawshank Redemption* that stuck with me. "It really only comes down to one choice... you either get busy living or get busy dying." I try to focus on the fact that Christmas isn't about me and how selfish it is to even take any time to feel sorry for myself. It's Jesus's Birthday! It's really the only thing that matters.

For those of you reading this because you personally have not faced a tragedy but want to help someone who has, I can offer some advice. I wanted to talk about my sister. I wanted people to ask me how I was doing. When people ignored me, I felt as if Kristie's memory was fading and no one cared. Be there to listen. The awkwardness will fade once you open up and talk and you don't need to solve all their problems or have a magical answer for them. If nothing else, give them a copy of this book. The cards, texts, social media posts, and emails that I receive on Kristie's birthday and anniversary of her death are special because it gives me a sense that someone other than myself remembers. I love it when people share a memory with me about how Kristie impacted their life or made them laugh. If the pain of the loss is still raw, and you have not attended the funeral yet, instead of sending cut flowers, send a perennial plant that will continue to grow and live outside as the years pass. Cut flowers eventually die and there's just something depressing about seeing that process when your senses are heightened. Also, those tropical plants look nice but honestly, they have to be watered every day which is more effort than a person grieving needs.   If you don't like the idea of getting a plant then buy something unique or significant that will show them that you put some thought into it. Mom still has a bouquet of fake flowers in her hallway that she received after the funeral. I remember it well because it had a little birdhouse in it with dragon flies. A Christmas ornament is another suggestion, one of those little picture frames that you could put their loved ones photo in it. They probably won't hang it up this year, but they will appreciate it when they do get the courage to put up their Christmas tree again.

Then Jesus said, "Come to me, all of you who are weary and carry heavy burdens, and I will give you rest. Take my yoke upon you. Let me teach you, because I am humble and gentle at heart, and you will find rest for your souls. For my yoke is easy to bear, and the burden I give you is light."

~Matthew 11:28-30

6

Next there was the issue of anger, and I had a lot of it. Of course there were the obvious things I was angry about but also little stuff. When someone spelled her name wrong or was sharing a memory of her which I knew was inaccurate, I would get furious on the inside. It bothered me when people would say, "well she's an angel now", which is completely inaccurate. I know they meant well, but the Bible is very clear that we do not become angels when we die. We will actually be over the angels, so that irritated me. I thought of all the people that had treated her wrong in her life and the anger would just build up. I would cringe when I heard someone speak the name of the guy who murdered my sister. They could have been referring to a complete stranger who shared the same name, but I still hated it. I disguised my anger well, but inside. I was pretty vicious in my thoughts. My tongue was sharp and there were a lot of things I thought and said which I know were displeasing to God. The anger was relentless. When I was alone with my thoughts I would create scenarios in my head of someone disrespecting her memory and then think about how I would react to it, which would usually involve my inflicting bodily harm upon someone.

Being a Christian doesn't mean you aren't human. We are all living in these fleshy bodies and struggle with sin. I'm not proud of my behavior but I also know that God knew I was hurting. I've learned that anger is very dangerous and if you allow it to, it will consume you. You have to understand that there was a time that my family sat down together and discussed what we would do if he was not convicted and was released from jail. Did I mention that Dad was a Sunday school teacher for over twenty years? I'm glad we discussed our feelings and all the potential consequences for our actions. In the end, we put our faith in God and let Him take control. I really don't want to spend much time on the guy that murdered my sister and our experience in the courts because I know how frustrating it was. However, I know some of you are probably curious about what happened to him. After two years of going through the court system, he was charged as an adult. He pled guilty to first degree murder and larceny of her vehicle and was sentenced to life without the possibility of parole. Eight years later, while serving out his sentence, his life was brutally taken by another inmate. It's hard to talk about his death without sounding vindictive but it was a great relief for my family. Mom no longer had to worry about him someday getting out, or to think about what he was doing or if he'd been transferred. We no longer had to think of him in the present sense. He is forever a part of our lives and we can't change that, but it does make a difference if he is alive or just a bad memory. I remember exactly where I was and what I was doing when I got the call that he was dead. It's one of those things that I don't expect you to understand unless you've walked in my shoes. We learned very quickly that, inside the courtroom, the victim and the victim's family have absolutely no rights. It's all about the convicted. We were frustrated when we were told we couldn't even wear a pin with Kristie's picture on it on our clothes. We couldn't do anything that might sway a jury in our favor. It was difficult when we learned that the only photos that the jury would ever see of our beloved Kristie were crime scene photos. They wouldn't see her when she was alive and laughing. She was a real person. I felt like someone only looking at crime scene photos wasn't getting the full picture. It would be easy to create distance from those bloody pictures and not want to think that at one time that was a real person. If you think about it, had she been injured, she would have been allowed to sit in the courtroom and defend herself. Since she was dead, they wouldn't allow anything, not even a photo of her while she was alive to be present. It was sickening and just wrong. One of the positive things that came out of our court experience is that we were able to get a bill passed in her name. It's called the Kristie LeGrange Bill, HB 2216, and it was passed in 2002. The Kristie LeGrange Bill says that an 8 X 10 photo of the "living" victim is allowed during the sentencing phase of the trial. It's a small victory for Oklahoma law but it means a great deal to the victim's family.

I'm not going to lie, from time to time the anger tries to resurface and I have to face it again but it gets easier each time. I have found ways to release it such as throwing on some workout clothes and going for a long walk, or having a lengthy talk with the Lord and just giving it all to Him to carry for me. No matter what the means, I don't allow it to consume me. I've seen stories on TV where a victim's family or maybe just one family member will become good friends with the murderer over time. That option was not for me. I don't think this means I'm a horrible Christian or that someone else is a better Christian because they did. I go back to the fact that people differ in how they grieve and overcome it. The troubling thing is that I knew exactly what my sister would say. She would tell me to forgive him, not necessarily because she cared about him, but because she loved me. I believe there is a big misconception regarding forgiveness. I don't believe forgiving someone means you have to forget about what they did nor does it mean that you think their actions were acceptable. I think that's where a lot of people go wrong. They think there is no way they are ever going to forgive! Somehow they think that means they are accepting of what happened, and that's not it at all. You aren't dishonoring your loved one at all by saying you forgive someone. To me, it's a process of letting go of the anger surrounding it and saying "okay, I am going to move on now. I am no longer going to let this person who stole so much from me take any more of my time or of my life." There is healing and relief in doing that but it's not easy to get to that point, or it wasn't for me anyway. If you don't ever get there, then you will spend the rest of your life thinking about this person and fighting the anger over and over. The fact they are still breathing air every day when your loved one is not, is enough. We were fortunate to be part of a homicide support group. These were individuals that really did know what we were going through. They helped in our journey, not just emotionally, but with the process as well. We received reports on where the murderer was being held and anytime he was going to be transferred. I could also go online and pull up his mug shots. I will warn you that seeing the photos of his face had its pros and cons.

I also had a great deal of anger for the agency she worked for and blamed their lousy policies and greed for not protecting her better. My feelings toward them are still strong, but more so because I worry about the process and the fact that not much has changed. There are so many people in occupations that require them to risk their lives by going into people's homes to help them. Nurses, physical therapists, and counselors are just a few examples. I understand completely that the types of people that choose to do this are givers. They love helping other people. It's honorable, but I don't understand why it can't be made safer for them. Kristie definitely didn't do it for the money, because she made just enough to cover her bills. She received her reward in other ways. It was the success stories that made her day, the ones where she made a difference. There has to be a better way to handle things than pushing the employees to get in more hours and sending them out before they even have all of the records on the patient. How can they help someone or know what they're getting into if they don't know their complete history. I could go on and on about this, but I won't bore you. The truth is that the number of deaths that do occur aren't high enough to make enough people care enough to demand change or they are kept quiet of fear of drawing too much attention to their broken procedures.

I don't know how many people have to die before someone says, maybe it's not a good idea to send a young beautiful girl out by herself to the home of a mentally unstable person. The bigger question for me is why in the world would you send someone in there and not allow them to protect themselves? We don't send our police officers into situations armed with only a cell phone and a policy book that says in case of an emergency call 911. They are trained for intense situations and are confident that if the situation arises, they have the ability to defend themselves. My message to the agencies out there that have a staff of counselors would be to care about your employees first. Make sure they have everything they need before you assign them a client. Give them the tools to do the best job possible and the training they need so that at least they have a chance to defend themselves. I think you will be surprised by your results.

Wait for the Lord; be strong and take heart and wait for the Lord.

~Psalm 27:14

7

There was a window of time right after her death when I found myself confused because I couldn't remember where in the Bible it talked about when she would actually get to heaven. I would spend an entire day analyzing the events and how they played out and I wanted to know exactly where she was and what the Bible said about it. The more I thought about it, the more I started to worry. I worried that maybe her spirit was stuck in transit until Jesus returned or in some sort of slumber until she's awakened by the angels transporting her. I knew that wasn't right, but I wasn't thinking straight and couldn't remember the actual passages where this was discussed. Finally, I asked Dad. I've always looked to my father when it came to God's word because he studied it regularly and in my mind he knew everything. I try to be diligent in my daily reading of the Bible but I have not been as disciplined as he has been. He seems to always have the answers when I ask. He brought peace to my heart when he said "Do you remember what Jesus said to the thief when he was hanging on the cross? He told him that today you will be with me in paradise. He didn't say in five years or when I return, He said today". That was exactly what I needed to hear. If your loved one was a Christian then you can be sure that at the moment of death, he/she was immediately ushered into the presence of the Lord. I liked that verse so much that we put that on her headstone as well.

We weren't able to have an open casket funeral for Kristie because of the trauma to her face, but the funeral home director built a special veil that covered the damage while still allowing us to say our goodbyes. I'm sure everyone has different opinions about this, but for me the viewing was what finalized the fact that it was real. To me, it was important to see her and say goodbye. I remember when we were kids, Kristie got really upset that we buried the family dog before she made it home from school. She would bring it up from time to time, making sure we didn't forget that she didn't get to see Peewee and have proper closure. She was a therapist even as a kid. When we got out of the car that evening and were walking to the front door of the funeral home, I glanced in one of the windows and, through the lacey curtains I saw her. There in her white casket with angels adorning the corners was my sister's dead body. I just stopped and stared through the glass. The last time I saw her she was alive and full of life. Shopping and laughing, we were both excited about the future. When I opened the door to the funeral home, I was greeted with more flowers than I could have ever imagined. Flowers lined the hallway and were overflowing her room. It was quite an amazing site of love. I walked slowly, taking it all in, forcing myself to go into the room where she lay. My Mother was crying and had brought some white house slippers to put on her feet. We each took turns spending some time alone with her. I focused on her hands it made me angry to see all the scratches and cuts. I wanted to look at her feet again, because her second toe curled under a little and I always made fun of it. Seeing those unique features, there was no doubt it was her. Crying I started to talk to her, even though I knew she wasn't there. I leaned down very close to the veil to whisper in her ear when I smelled the embalming fluid. It was at that moment that I realized she wasn't coming back, and I told her I was mad at her for leaving me. I told her she was a liar when she promised she'd always be there for me. I told her I was sorry and that I should have been there with her to stop him. You have to understand; I would have stopped him or died trying.

When I reflect back on the funeral, the things I remember the most are the things most would say were insignificant: the fact they ran out of space in the family book for signatures, so people started signing their names on napkins, how the Church's sign which was normally filled with a funny saying or verse simply read the words "Jesus Wept," the attendance of a group of firemen dressed in their full uniforms. The outpouring of love for our family was overwhelming. While riding to the grave side, I peered out the window watching the trees pass in a blur. I caught a glimpse of two young boys who pulled their bikes over to the side of the road and stopped out of respect for the funeral procession. Holding their baseball hats over their hearts, they watched as the hearse drove by. Those boys don't realize that their small gesture of kindness made a mark on my heart forever.

I've been asked before if I felt suicidal after Kristie's death and although I admit I did think about it, I never considered it a real option. As a Christian, I believe when I go through a storm, one of the key factors of having faith is trusting that God will see me through it and in the process teach me and mold me into a stronger person. I'll admit I wanted to die so I could be with her again but not through suicide. Everyone I know has somehow been touched by someone that has committed suicide and it's very painful for those left behind. You have to think of others. I understand wanting the pain to stop, but if you are a Christian and are not suffering from any mental illness, you are risking God's stiff judgment for taking your life. God knows your heart and I promise you that if you give it to God, He will get you through. No one said it would be easy.

Jesus answered him, "I tell you the truth, today you will be with me in paradise."

~Psalm 27:14

8

I found myself asking what possible good can come from this tragedy. How can I take this situation and somehow turn this into good? It's something you don't want to do because there is nothing that can justify the loss, the death or the murder. At the same time you don't want his or her life to be in vain. As a family, we took donations and did some nice charity work in her honor, but I was still left with this feeling that her death wasn't justified. I can't give you an answer to that because there really isn't anything that can justify it. I was so consumed with seeing everything that I had lost, that for a long time I wasn't able to see the spiritual gain. So what does that mean? In the process of going through this trial, I acquired a very unique spiritual gift. Whether I like it or not, I now have this experience that I can use to witness, help, and share with others. I will find myself drawn to people that have had similar tragedies. I have gone through something that not many other people have gone through and with God's help, I witness to them, share my experience, or just listen. I don't think anyone wakes up and says they want to be part of the "my sister was murdered club." I am and I can't change that. I am thankful for those out there who had also gone through something tragic and took the time to share with me. Those shared experiences made me feel like I wasn't alone. I wasn't able to get that comfort from others that were just sympathetic. It feels different when someone else reaches out to you that has gone through what you are going through. Our world is so upside down and TV is a huge reminder of how so many people have their priorities all wrong. Everywhere you look there are people fighting over things that don't matter, not realizing how precious life is and how short the time here really is.

I mentioned before we were fortunate that a group called the Homicide Support Group reached out to us. Mom made a close friend and we were able to go on a tour of a prison as a group. We bonded and through that connection we found healing. It's funny because I refused to go to a grief counselor. I was so angry with her murderer that I refused to put myself in the same role he was in at the time of her death. I did not want to be the "client." Kristie would have wanted me to, but the best I could do was to go through a grief and loss program that my church offered. I am so glad I did because I found comfort with the ladies in my group. We cried together, laughed together, and healed together. I found inspiration in meeting others who had gone through horrible tragedies including some who had lost their entire family. They shared their journey and when I saw that they were able to make it, I knew that I could as well. All of our experiences were different but we shared similar pain and grief. There were definitely days I didn't want to attend but I was always glad once I got there and was happy afterwards that I had made myself go.

Besides watching what seemed like my parents aging overnight, I also witnessed the direct impact on their health. Mom struggled with constant stomach issues which doctors blamed on her nerves. One thing that really helped Mom was the large gazebo my father built in the backyard in Kristie's memory. It included a steeple on top with stained glass that lit up at night. Kristie had quite the collection of crosses and also little churches. Whether it was a glass figurine or a birdhouse shaped like a church, she loved them. This is where my Father drew his inspiration for the design. I noticed Mom became quite the homebody after Kristie's death. She lacked the desire to go anywhere for a long time, but after Dad built the gazebo, it wasn't long before she started coming out of the house more. Each day she spent a little more time outside weeding and planting flowers around it.   There are also numerous sets of wind chimes that she hung nearby. She must hear the same bittersweet music in the chimes that I do.

For a long time, Kristie was always the first thing I thought of when I woke up and the last thing on my mind before I cried myself to sleep.   After two years and all the court proceedings were finally over, I felt like I was getting my life back together. Shortly after that, the State returned my sister's personal items which had been held for evidence. A zip-lock bag held her clothes, which looked brown from the dried blood, and her jewelry, which was smashed almost completely flat. I couldn't help but stare at them. A couple of them had been cut, I assume because they couldn't get them off her fingers. These details really added to the visual of her last moments.   I kept these things and put them in a cedar chest. It may seem weird, but from time to time I open it up and look through her special things. It's painful, but there is healing in the pain. It took time but I did have some feeling of normalcy again. I think for most, the thought of moving on has a negative vibe attached to it because it sounds selfish. I can tell you that moving on did not mean I forgot about what happened. It is with you every day, my friend. We can't change that, it's just part of life. The void in your life, that place where the person you lost gave you joy, will never be the same. I have two children now, while my kids have brought me years of happiness, it is a different kind of happiness. No person or thing can replace the kind of joy that Kristie brought to me. She could make me laugh so hard I would cry. We could finish each other's sentences. We knew each other as well as we knew ourselves. There is just something special about a sister that cannot be explained. If you have a sibling, you might know what I'm talking about. We were each other's best friend and although God has given me other forms of joy and happiness, that special joy she brought to my life will never be replaced. I look forward to seeing her again. I smile picturing that moment when God reunites us and know as I move forward, it gets a little closer.

I know everyone is different and may not experience the same phases of grief as I did, but it's worth mentioning that I experienced a time where I believed I was cursed. I put up an imaginary wall preventing anyone from getting too close to me or allowing myself to meet any new friends. Like a turtle in its shell, I pulled in my head and kept to myself. Kristie was my best friend and no one would ever replace her so why even try to build relationships that would always be in her shadow? Plus, I feared for those around me. The ones I dearly loved could be at risk. If the devil found out how much I loved them, then he would continue his mission to destroy me by taking their lives as well. To this day, I still have a wall up but it's shorter now. I'll eventually let those in that are persistent and patient with me. Now I'm glad when I get to meet new people. I have found when I open up to others, I find we have more in common and I like to believe that God has somehow crossed our paths for a reason.

I hope somehow in reading this book, you have been able to take away something that has brought you comfort. I know that going forward is not easy, but if you take it one day at time, each step gets a little easier. If you don't try, then the Devil has already won. Don't give him the pleasure of knowing that what he took away from you has forced you to question your faith and your purpose in this life. Use your anger in a positive way so that your storm strengthens you and builds perseverance. I like to think of the trials we face as God's way of tapping us on the shoulder and saying "Hey, do I have your attention now? You need to look at Me." God has a plan for you, which may not always make sense, but I can tell you one thing for certain, I've read the Book and I know how it ends. He is always in control and in the end we will be victorious.

Blessed be the God and Father of our Lord Jesus Christ, the Father of mercies and God of all comfort; who comforts us in all our affliction so that we may be able to comfort those who are in any affliction with the comfort with which we ourselves are comforted by God.

~2 Corinthians 1:3-4

Final Thoughts

There was a time in Kristie's life when she was engaged to be married. Although the marriage was called off, at the time, I remember being overwhelmed with the thought of losing my sister. I believed her marriage would change our relationship, and she and I would no longer get to spend the same amount of time together. One evening I felt driven to write something that I could read to her at the wedding to show her how deep my affection was for her. As I've said before, there are no words that can describe the bond between sisters. I remember kneeling at the edge of my bed, crying as I wrote the words, the poem that I later called "Souled." It was a curious thing that, while I wrote this poem, I sensed this was more fitting for a funeral than a wedding. I truly believe in my heart that I was guided by the Holy Spirit that night, years before her actual death. As my tears and words poured out, maybe I was somehow being prepared for what was to come. In front of an overflowing church I read my poem at her funeral. At the graveside service as people were walking through shaking our hands and consoling us, a young man placed a penny in my hand. Every visit to the cemetery, there on her headstone we would find pennies. At one point, Mom put a little metal bucket out there because there were so many pennies you couldn't see the headstone. It was touching to say the least.

Souled

I held in my hands a penny once, a new copper penny that's value was great,

For now it is mine for the keeping, but I cannot determine its fate.

Priority was my penny; the penny always came first,

With me the penny went everywhere, together we conquered the worst.

I kept it safe in my pocket, where I knew it would never be lost,

I would not spend it, not ever, or my heart would pay the cost.

Occasionally I'd take out of my pocket my penny, to just stare at it in awe,

To everyone else it was just a penny, but to me, the most beautiful sight I ever saw.

Although my penny aged, and its shiny coat turned bronze with time,

I would not trade it for a new one, not for five, or even a dime.

I feared those that might take my penny, so I guarded it with all my might,

But one day something happened and I felt things weren't quite right.

My penny no longer needed me, to keep it safe and secured,

My penny was ready to be spent, the stock had finally matured.

I knew that the time was near, so slowly I closed my eyes,

My penny that was once clenched in my hand was held open now to the skies.

Today I decided to turn over, what was valued greatly by many,

Today I leave it behind, and in God's hand I lay my penny.

But Ruth replied, "Don't urge me to leave you or to turn back from you. Where you go I will go, and where you stay I will stay. Your people will be my people and your God my God. Where you die I will die, and there I will be buried. May the Lord deal with me, be it ever so severely, if even death separates you and me."

~Ruth 1:16-19

Resources:

* Check with your local church to see if they offer a Grief & Loss Recovery class

* Contact me via email - michellewalker99@cox.net

www.ingramcontent.com/pod-product-compliance
Lightning Source LLC
Chambersburg PA
CBHW062125040426
42337CB00044B/4263